IMPERFECTLY PERFECT

AUTISM REDEFINED
Krista-Marie's Story

by

Dr. Bernardo Gonzalez

Marta Gonzalez

Copyright © 2019 Bernardo Gonzalez
All rights reserved.

Krista-Marie's essence and legacy:
To Truly Live each moment
To genuinely Love the world around us
To joyfully Laugh to make a difference
And enjoy Life to its fullest

Krista and Coco-Chanel

PREFACE
(A LETTER TO OUR DAUGHTER)

Dear Krista,

On April 12, 2000, you blessed our family with the presence of your beautiful soul. You were our second daughter, possessed a unique personality wonderfully shaped and unhindered by an unbalanced ego or self-imposed delusions—a personality fully immersed in the manifestation of unconditional love. Most importantly, anyone who watched you saw a perfect roadmap to living life. I wrote this book to share your essence and story.

In my life, I have met and spoken with thousands of mothers and fathers. I never met one that hoped they would outlive their child, but it happens. When it does, all the hoping in the world cannot change it. I have often heard those same mommies and daddies say, "I don't care if it is a boy or a girl, as long as the baby is healthy." Mom and I wished that for you as well; but you came to us just as you were, imperfectly perfect. The doctors explained that what you had is called *autism*, or *autism spectrum disorder* (ASD). It is a broad range of conditions characterized by challenges with social skills, repetitive behaviors, speech, and nonverbal communication. You were not the only child born with it, because one in fifty-nine children in this country has some form of it. Mom and I hoped you would outlive us, but that was not to be. Krista, although you are no longer here, the memories of your smiles and hugs live on in our thoughts of you. You were and will always be our imperfectly perfect child, and our lives are better because you were a part of them.

    With thankful hearts!

    Mom and Dad

Chapter 1
Essential Building Blocks

Katrina, our oldest daughter, would pray on her knees at the side of her bed for a baby sister. Her Christmas wish list always had a baby sister on it. The question in our mind as parents was, should we adopt? Gratefully, her bond with two of her cousins, Javier and Erica, played a big role to fill the missing void she felt in her heart. Together with her incredible grandparents ("Mamama" and "Ata") and cousins, we united as a family on regular beach outings and Disney trips.

As a family, we already had a beautiful little girl named Katrina when my wife became pregnant with twins. One day, my wife called and told me that she was rushing to the hospital because there was something wrong with the twins. Upon her reaching the hospital, she had a miscarriage, and that loss would not be the only trial my family would have to endure. I recall crying while I hugged my daughter Katrina, and although, because of her young age, I never told her the reason I was crying, her presence, affection, and love made all the difference in the world.

Emotions should be shared with people you love.

We received the impactful news from doctors that we could not have any more children.

As parents, we concentrated on loving and caring for our daughter and talked about early retirement. My wife left her lucrative job and started an insurance consulting business out of the house so she could dedicate more time to our only daughter.

As a family, we harnessed strength and persevered.

I worked full time and started teaching at universities to offset the loss of my wife's income. Although the miscarriage was a sad and traumatic event, as a family we felt blessed to have each other. It was a wonderful time and a beautiful life.

My daughter flourished and bloomed into an amazing eight-year-old. The years passed, and the thought of having another child became a distant afterthought. However, our Creator had other plans for our family.

Valuable Lessons Learned:

- ***Emotions should be shared with people you love.***
- ***As a family we harnessed strength, adapted, and persevered.***

Chapter 2
Life's Unexpected Gift

I remember coming home from work one day and observing my wife sitting on our bed. She delivered the news that we were going to have another baby. The news hit me unexpectedly, and I recalled thinking of what the doctors had advised us after losing the twins.

In the game of life, science sometimes doesn't hold all the answers.

My wife's pregnancy was considered high-risk, but thankfully the pregnancy went well until the time of delivery. The baby was under tremendous stress and was not receiving the proper oxygen level required. The doctor's eyes were conveying two messages: we have serious complications with the baby, and the look of doubt that maybe she should have performed a cesarean earlier.

I have come to learn by experience that the saying, "The eyes are the windows to the soul," is as close to an absolute truth as anything I have seen.

No religious position, perceived reality, or personal ideology could have prepared us for what was to come. The great challenges in our lives cannot be overcome or solved by elaborate speeches, spiritual facades, or forced personal positioning.

The battle scars of life, if we traverse through the pain and seek the truth, can serve to redirect or correct one's misguided fixed positions.

Once our daughter Krista was born, she was rushed to an intensive care unit and placed in an oxygenated incubator. She was also given heavy antibiotics intravenously due to developing an acute infection (as a result of remaining in a stressful environment for an exceedingly long period of time). My wife and I were forced to endure the horrible possibility that our newborn baby might not be a part of our family for much longer. During our regular hospital visits, I remember having to explain to Katrina that her baby sister was very sick. As I look back now, I can see what I did not see then, different characterizations of suffering occurring simultaneously:

- A parent's fear of the unknown with plenty of questions and absolutely no answers
- A sister's fear of the world around her, affecting her very essence of security and control
- A newborn's fear of having to endure so much pain from the moment of conception

This suffering would prove to be a crucial component of our family's very essence, the essence of survival.

One thing is for certain: the suffering endured helped shaped the character trait of perseverance for all participants (mother, father, sister, and newborn).

Valuable Lessons Learned:

- *In the game of life, science sometimes doesn't hold all the answers.*
- *I have come to learn by experience that the saying, "The eyes are the windows to the soul," is as close to an absolute truth as anything I have seen.*
- *The battle scars of life, if we traverse through the pain and seek the truth, can serve to redirect or correct one's misguided fixed positions.*

Chapter 3
Love Should Not Be Controlled by Human Understanding

Krista-Marie was a fighter and adapted to harsh treatments and experimental procedures with a sense of acceptance and trust in her family. No matter the hardships that she endured, a smile followed to let us know that the procedure or treatment did not have a lasting impact on her essence.

It is here where my mentor's (Krista's) story begins. I still remember being in the hospital and the doctor telling my wife and me that Krista had spinal meningitis and would never walk. At that very moment, our thoughts of the past or future abruptly came to an end. The only thing that had any importance was the acute realization of the present moment and our youngest daughter's condition. My wife began to process the idea of wheelchairs and setting up the house so it would meet her needs, while I stared at the parking lot of the hospital in a desperate attempt to connect to my inner essence and spirit, with the distant hope of finding a way.

Life's answers can only be realized by walking in the present. And the present is ever changing, for a day later, the same doctor came running to our hospital room with the news that the test results were negative, and that our youngest daughter did not have spinal meningitis.

At that moment, Krista was still in critical condition with all sorts of antibiotics and fluids being pumped intravenously. In addition, she endured several spinal taps to ensure the infection had not traveled through her spinal cord. Her body and little head bore the scars of the needles. One day, as I was visiting the intensive care unit, a nurse commented, "I will let you hold her if you promise to stay holding her for at least thirty minutes. If you don't have the courage and can't muster it, don't do it because it will not be worth it for her." This would prove to be a pivotal moment in my life. Consciously and with all my essence, I engaged in the present. ***The present can only be engaged as an act of consciousness.***

I remembered holding her and staring at this innocent baby, thinking to myself how enduring this kind of pain so early in life could alter someone's personality and state of being for a lifetime. The thought of her never smiling came to my mind as I began to sing a made-up lullaby to her. As she listened, ***she looked into my eyes with a gaze so piercing and so powerful that it reached the deepest core of my being. A person knows that they have reached this level of depth when everything about them (thoughts and inner being) grows extremely clear and the truth of events*** *become genuinely transparent. It is as if for a moment, I could experience in my daughter's gaze the truth and very nature of God's spirit.* For twelve wonderful years, this lesson and powerful gaze would prove to be a common theme in my life. I could not have been more wrong about my daughter never smiling. Krista's permanent radiant and profound smile, along with her ability to persevere through complex and extremely hard situations, would become her very mantra of existence.

She came home from the hospital hooked up to a machine with intravenous lines pumping antibiotics to relieve a variety of infections. She also came home with the following conditions:

- Bones of her skull deformed
- Skin continuously developing a thick layer of crust that covered her little body
- Problem with the bones of her legs and feet
- Problems with muscle tone development throughout her body
- Problems with her sensory development
- Problems with swallowing, due to the tubes placed in her throat
- Learning disabilities (autism and apraxia to name a few of her genetic struggles)

Even early on in her life, it became apparent that my daughter had a unique and extraordinary personality and essence. Most amazing for me was how she began to radiate joy for life as she commenced to persevere through all her struggles. Krista never allowed the hardships she endured to take away her love and zest for life. ***Life's essence and value can only be defined and measured by our Creator's definition.***

Valuable Lessons Learned:

- *Life's answers can only be realized by walking in the present.*
- *The present can only be engaged as an act of consciousness.*
- *She looked into my eyes with a gaze so piercing and so powerful that it reached the deepest core of my being. A person knows that they have reached this level of depth when everything about them (thoughts and inner being) grows extremely clear and the truth of events become genuinely transparent. Is as if for a moment, I could experience in my daughter's gaze the truth and very nature of God's spirit.*
- *Life's essence and value can only be defined and measured by our Creator's definition.*

Chapter 4
The Power of the Present

Who really has a disability in life? Krista-Marie's sense of joy was simple; she had no problem walking up to a stranger and smiling or just giving them a hug.

Don't get me wrong, she picked up negative energy too and knew how to distinguish it. One day Krista-Marie was sitting inside the grocery cart, and while I was paying, she gently touched the elderly employee's face that was assisting with our groceries. My instinct was to pull her hand.

Naturally, I did not want her touching a stranger's face, but then I looked at the man's emotional reaction, and he just looked at me and said, "No one has ever touched me like that." He just looked at me and then smiled at Krista-Marie. I left there with mixed feelings: I'm so conditioned to protect her from strangers, but she just touched this poor little old man's heart, and who was I to stop that? Encounters like these continued throughout her life.

Life offers no certainty; individuals who grasp this reality of existence understand the meaning and truth of the present. I sometimes think that society lives in a constant state of illusion, an appearance of what we wish to be true. Our habits, patterns of thought, and actions offer us the perfect veneer of security. We go through life with the erroneous perception of having complete control of the events around us. However, in time life will always remind us of how little control we really have.

In these moments, we come to understand that the only partial control we have is in the reality of the present moment.

The realization of this truth can have a liberating and positive influence in one's life. Failure to realize this truth can lead us to prioritize our life incorrectly.

Our self-imposed habits and actions push us to center our lives in the past or future, creating a veneer of false security, that if allowed, distances us from the joy of living.

It is here where I believe we choke out the essence and truth of the present. We extinguish the only possible chance to live life according to its original design and purpose. In our family's case, the coming of Krista was a gift, a gift that grounded us to live in the present moment and did not allow us to wallow in the past or future. A gift that I want to share, cherish, and actively pursue for the rest of my life.

My daughter possessed these traits in the most natural and instinctive manner. She never acquired this gift from reading the Tao, Buddhist or Hindu writings, Koran, Torah, or Bible. ***She*** *lived naturally, perfectly in tune with her spirit.* Her personality blossomed through the years amazingly fine-tuning her innate nature. It is difficult for me to comprehend how she could maintain a positive disposition and constant state of joy while enduring so much pain and hardship.

It is common for children possessing severe learning disabilities, especially with their speech and motor skills, to become frustrated and aggressive from their inability to express their desires and emotions.

These feelings of distress are usually augmented in children that are mentally aware of their surroundings and possess a clear sense of purpose regarding their wants and desires. The emotional pain of being unable to communicate verbally and physically their wants and desires creates a buildup of anguish and frustration. I have seen children caught in this emotional vise express themselves aggressively and with great distress. Children suffering from this horror, as an escape, begin to withdraw from the world around them. The action of withdrawing due to their inability to express and satisfy their basic needs and desires, can manifest into a state of sadness and depression. My daughter was caught in this vise, possessing a clear sense of purpose regarding her wants and desires and yet being unable to communicate them verbally to the world around her. However, due to her unique God-given personality and extraordinary ability to fight and persevere, she never exhibited feelings of sadness, depression, and aggressiveness. Instead, her personality flourished by consistently expressing and radiating a sense of joy and happiness. I am still amazed at her ability to do this. How can someone enduring so much pain and suffering be so amazingly happy and cheerful all the time? ***The mixture of Love and Perseverance is a powerful mixture to live by!***

Valuable Lessons Learned:

- *In the harshest trials, we come to understand that the only partial control we have is in the reality of the present moment.*
- *Our self-imposed habits and actions push us to center our lives in the past or future, creating a veneer of false security, that if allowed, distances us from the joy of living.*
- *She lived naturally, perfectly in tune with her spirit.*
- *The mixture of Love and Perseverance is a powerful mixture to live by.*

Chapter 5
Unequal Equilibrium

I never understood the impact a special needs child would have for our family. Yes, I gave to charity and I was compassionate toward those in need, but I was not aware of what life was like for anyone with special needs. More frustrating is when you don't have a clear diagnosis of what is happening to your daughter. As a parent, at that moment you are clueless and have no idea where to start. Krista-Marie contradicted medical theories related to her condition consistently. The baby books that I kept searching for were on typical children. I'm a big believer that "experience" can be considered to be life's university, providing an extremely strong base of knowledge that often cannot be obtained through books. So... I started engaging with other mothers and therapists that dealt with hands-on situations with children in situations like Krista-Marie's. Labeling a child was a double-edge sword and not the answer. The only true thing that mattered was what we did as parents and how we assisted our child in getting stronger. The answer, to us, went back to parents' and therapists' knowledge and experience. Patience was crucial during the frustrating days where we took three steps forward and two steps back.

Regardless, you were one step ahead toward progress.

Our family structure revolved around trying to achieve a state of unequal equilibrium. As I have named it, **unequal equilibrium is sort of finding perfection in imperfection.** *The theory appears to conflict, but just like the concept of synergy (synergy being greater than the sum of the individual parts) equilibrium is reached by the sum of the unequal parts reaching a state of a healthy balance.* A state of healthy balance that is centered in the following important areas:

- Valuing, caring for, and providing attention to all family members

- Family members providing maximum value, care, and attention to the family member requiring the most need

After several spinal taps and countless uncomfortable and painful medical procedures, my daughter left the hospital. I still remember her crying when they were removing a large medical tape stuck to her back. It was a sound that we almost never heard again. During her twelve years with us, she seldom cried. She battled and fought through her physical and emotional shortcomings, but seldom cried.

Krista came home immediately fighting to overcome her limitations. *What we did not know then is that she never looked at herself as having any limitations. In her eyes, and I firmly believe in the eyes of her Creator, she was perfect. Perfect to teach the family and people around her so many lessons.* Lessons that can still be learned today for whoever is whiling to see them. She struggled to make small movements in her crib. She struggled and struggled so hard until she persevered. She struggled to turn her body from her back to her stomach. My daughter tried and tried until she conquered the movement.

She couldn't crawl but mastered moving around on her stomach. She endured countless scrubbings to remove dry fluid her body continuously secreted. She endured the pain (she screamed) with remarkable courage, never letting the process impact her personality in a negative fashion. I still don't know how she was able to do this (she feared and hated the scrubbings.) She endured a special helmet placed securely on her to fix the disfigured bones of her skull.

She persevered through countless medical procedures such as hyperbaric oxygen chambers, operation, a small balloon inserted inside her nose to push her uneven skull in place, special equipment to align the bones of her feet and legs, countless vials of blood, X-rays, scans, and daily physical, occupational, speech, and behavior therapies. It is perplexing how a child can endure so much and remain so joyful and full of life. *Most important, she lived totally in the present, withdrawing the marrow and essence of life moment by moment. She did not get bogged down with the sorrow and pain of the past and never allowed the future to tarnish the joy of the present moment.* What a beautiful life! What a beautiful and powerful human being!

My God, I miss her so much! I too must learn from her. *My daughter's mantra: endure, persevere, and at all cost, don't allow anything to steal the joy of your present moment!*

Valuable Lessons Learned:

- *Unequal equilibrium is sort of finding perfection in imperfection.*
- *She lived totally in the present, withdrawing the marrow and essence of life moment by moment.*
- *What we did not know then is that she never looked at herself as having any limitations. In her eyes, and I firmly believe in the eyes of her Creator, she was perfect.*
- *She did not get bogged down with the sorrow and pain of the past and never allowed the future to tarnish the joy of the present moment.*
- *My daughter's mantra: endure, persevere, and at all cost, don't allow anything to steal the joy of your present moment!*

Chapter 6
Follower of Christ

Strolling through the mall was one of Krista-Marie's favorite pastimes with Mom. We always entered through the Dillard's store and then had a few highlighted locations that were a must! One was a train ride by the food court. Krista-Marie loved to take several turns on the train, and the lady that attendant loved to see her expression on the train. One day after the train and on our way to our special place, the Disney Store, Krista-Marie locked hands with a beautiful lady wearing her traditional hijab.

At first, I was surprised and tried to have Krista-Marie let go. My initial thought was that Krista-Marie had done something inappropriate, but I quickly picked up a vibe that was completely unusual and unexpected. I noticed that they were not only staring straight into each other's eyes, but also were holding hands.

As a mother, I felt like there was a connection and I was a separate entity. I was an outsider in their connection. The lady looked at me with a very piercing look and smiled as she said, "It looks like you were given an angel." They exchanged looks again, and then she said, "You are very lucky and have been chosen," and walked away.

I continued to our next destination, which was the Disney Store. There, Krista-Marie ran off to study all the wonderful items and the movie screen playing a Disney cartoon. I was mesmerized by what I had experienced. Immediately, I had to call Bernie and share, but words could not express the moment.

The name Krista means "anointed follower of Christ." And it is clear to see how my daughter's life resembles His:

- Christ endured unimaginable suffering. (Krista endured inconceivable suffering throughout her life.)

- Christ suffered unfairness and was ridiculed by society. (Krista endured constant unfairness and ridicule from the so-called normal world around her.)
- Christ suffered systemic injustice. (Krista lived in a system that did not understand her learning disabilities and created countless obstacles that attempted to hamper her growth and development.)
- Christ persevered through inconceivable odds. (Krista persevered through unimaginable trials that would have destroyed the strongest of persons.)
- Christ was fully connected and fused to God's spirit. (I believe that Krista was innately and

naturally fused to her Creator in ways that cannot be logically explained or comprehended.)

- Christ incessantly loved unconditionally. (Krista effortlessly loved unconditionally.)
- Christ lived in the present with practical simplicity. (Krista was a master of knowing how to live in the present moment with model practicality and simplicity.)
- Christ died abruptly at the age of thirty-three with only three years of recorded history. (Krista only lived twelve years on this earth.)
- Christ's love continues to shine and make a difference in people's life. (Krista's Love is a

guiding light and powerful force for those that want to see it.)

- Christ's manner of living continues to teach and inspire our thoughts and actions. (Along with Christ, I consider Krista my greatest teacher.)
- Christ was and is a light that inspired and is still inspiring people. (Krista motivated and is motivating, inspired and is inspiring people from all walks of life.)
- Christ found eternal peace. (It is my belief that Krista is in a perfect and unexplained relation with her Creator in a state of perfect peace unknown to human beings.)

Valuable Lessons Learned:

- *Christ was fully connected and fused to God's spirit. (I believe that Krista was innately and naturally fused to her Creator in ways that cannot be logically explained or comprehended.)*
- *Christ lived in the present with practical simplicity. (Krista was a master of knowing how to live in the present moment with model practicality and simplicity.)*
- *Christ was and is a light that inspired and is still inspiring people. (Krista motivated and is motivating, inspired and is inspiring people from all walks of life.)*
- *Christ found eternal peace. (It is my belief that Krista is in a perfect and unexplained relation with her Creator in a state of perfect peace unknown to human beings.*

Chapter 7
The Wasteful Attitude of Self Pity

It is incredible how you learn about people's behavior and insecurities when you are in the world of a special needs child. I used to tell my daughter Katrina, "God created us all equal; he just rearranged us with different patterns." We are all created equally. We all have some type of disability. Some are visible and some are not. However, for an eight-year-old child, understanding the meaning of God's work can be extremely confusing.

As parents, we wanted to have all the answers, but the truth is that we did not understand certain things happening to us in the journey. Katrina was sandwiched between day-to-day uncertainties and trying to understand her own emotions somehow. (We will examine Katrina's story and courage in Chapter 15.e)

There is nothing more wasteful and unproductive than the attitude of self-pity. I describe *self-pity* as generating the conditions of being inside a never-ending spin cycle. Problems keep rotating and rotating in one's mind without any sign of progress or intent to resolve the given situation. Moreover, **self-pity erodes the very fabric of integrity and truth.** More importantly, the truth related to the trial or tribulation being faced is concealed. ***The concealment of this truth alters growth and the awareness of any positive outcome.*** This self-defeating spin cycle almost always produces fear and anxiety, altering an individual's quest of finding peace of mind.

Krista did not live in the world of self-pity. She never felt sorry for herself, and equally important did not live in the world of needing people to feel sorry for her. She lived in the here and now, with a natural essence of perfectly balanced priorities. ***Krista's priorities centered on radiating love and making a real difference to the people around her.*** I always find intriguing individuals who pay more attention to the distant sorrow far removed from them than to the family members and friends close to them whom they frequent daily. Krista loved and cared about the people she touched every day. *Her circle of influence grew proportionally as the people she touched began to love and care in the same manner.* What natural God-given beauty and wisdom!

Valuable Lessons Learned:

- *There is nothing more wasteful and unproductive than the attitude of self-pity.*
- *Self-pity erodes the very fabric of integrity and truth.*
- *The concealment of truth alters growth and the awareness of any positive outcome.*
- *Krista's priorities centered on radiating love and making a real difference to the people around her.*
- *Her circle of influence grew proportionally as the people she touched began to love and care in the same manner.*

Chapter 8
Imperfectly Perfect

Every member of my family deeply loves me; however, I will never be loved by anyone so unconditionally as the way Krista-Marie loved. She had a special bond with each member of the family and naturally was able to radiate her love in the proportion and manner needed by the family member being engaged. She affected us each differently, with every member of the family clearly capturing and receiving the purity, honesty, and full transparency of her love. We had an incredible gift for twelve and a half years, and for this I will be eternally grateful.

I have been honored for twelve years to live side by side with pure love. This beautiful person has been and will continue to be my mentor, counselor, source of strength and inspiration. I have found my mentor's guidance particularly instrumental when the uncertainties and realities of life come crashing through one's doorstep. It is here, when we come face-to-face with our suffering and truth of existence, that we get a glimpse of our unfiltered makeup, essence, and character. Equally important, I find myself falling short when I measure myself alongside the measuring stick of my mentor's pure love.

In life, occurrences happen unexpectedly. The harshest blows of life almost always catch us by surprise. *When facing extremely difficult conditions, in most cases we feel useless and ineffective to alter our circumstances. This feeling of uselessness, if left unchecked, breeds a paralyzing fear and state of hopelessness.* It is here where we learn who we truly are. It is here where our true character is revealed.

Unchecked fear is the language of destruction.

In Buddhist thought, it is said that suffering is one of the four paths that lead an individual to enlightenment. Buddhism also mention that suffering should be viewed as a part of life, with its genesis commencing during our first days of existence. Buddhist writings teach us to accept suffering with patience and persevere in order to evolve in strength and courage.

During these times, our family was in a state of swim or sink, either persevere through the suffering or drown in the sorrow of uncertainty.

One thing can be said: the strength and courage of my daughter to endure and persevere through daunting odds gave our family the needed strength to continue loving life.

Valuable Lessons Learned:

- *When facing extremely difficult conditions, in most cases we feel useless and ineffective to alter our circumstances. This feeling of uselessness, if left unchecked, breeds a paralyzing fear and state of hopelessness.*
- *Unchecked fear is the language of destruction.*
- *During these times, our family was in a state of swim or sink, either persevere through the suffering or drown in the sorrow of uncertainty.*

Chapter 9
The Void Left Behind

Why would God expose me, teach me, and then take her away? God, why must I be in so much pain? Did I do something wrong? I tried to balance, serve, and love with all my heart. My life is now empty. I lost my teacher, my little buddy, and part of my soul.

I've lost my purpose. But... God placed some amazing people in my life, and one of them was my husband, Bernie. He sat me down one day and told me: "Before Krista-Marie, it was you, me, and Katrina; before Katrina, it was you and me; and before that, it was just you. You need to go into your heart and find out who you are."

How do you know when you really miss something?

The truth is that your very essence and spirit will communicate to you in unspoken words the fact that you truly miss something. ***The void and realization that you miss that something, in a manner more clearly than you could ever process it mentally, is so frightening and painful that the only word that comes to mind to describe it is the word* unimaginable.** It is only when traveling through this abyss that you truly know when you miss something. This feeling, in the deepest corridor of your essence, communicates to you in an extremely vivid, clear, and non-verbal manner how valuable the missing thing was for you. This is even more powerful when the missing thing happens to be your daughter.

I am sure that every father that has lost a child misses them. However, I firmly believe the void I am describing cannot be solely described as the pain of having lost a loved one, even if it is a child. I am certain of this: *the void is proportionate to the value of the life lost and what that life represented for you.* This void directly correlates to how the person (that has been lost) lived their life and the love that person radiated toward you. I humbly believe that this, in turn, helps to describe the nature, measure, and value of what is now missing.

Moreover, I firmly believe this to be true: what I have not said is that ***the antidote to the very real and horrible void is connecting to the very essence of the person that has departed.*** In my case this is connecting to the true nature, essence, and spirit of Krista. It is hard to comprehend the pleasure and peace of mind taking this action can generate. One thing I do know is, the inability to take this road properly can lead to acute pain, confusion, insecurity, and loss of joy.

When traversing through this kind of grief, I find it interesting how at times human beings frame things to feel better. People can be so certain that they hold the answer to your problem. Comments that sound good, for all intended purposes, might have a healthy motive but can still fail to reach their desired objective. Sometimes two comments exactly alike, said by two different people, can have completely different outcomes.

Only a person who is armed with the knowledge of the given situation and possesses the credibility to support such statement should voice their opinion. Individuals might mean well, but in my humble opinion, only those possessing the proper knowledge base on the situation being faced, along with the right motive, and credibility (to the person the message is being delivered) can make a difference to the intended person being afflicted by the trial or situation. Unless you possess these attributes (knowledge base, right motive, and credibility), it is probably best to remain silent!

Valuable Lessons Learned:
- *The void and realization that you miss that something, in a manner more clearly than you could ever process it mentally, is so frightening and painful that the only word that comes to mind to describe it is the word* **unimaginable.**
- *The void is proportionate to the value of the life lost and what that life represented for you.*
- *The antidote to the very real and horrible void is connecting to the very essence of the person that has departed.*
- *Only a person who is armed with the knowledge of the given situation and possesses the credibility to support such statement should voice their opinion.*

Chapter 10
The Process of Evolving

Losing Krista-Marie had taken all the color out of my life. Music sounded like shattered glass inside a blender. I felt alone in a room full of people. I did not feel like I belonged in a world of regular social gatherings. My world was hers, and she was still part of my soul; we had functioned every day like two separate bodies that integrated as one. However, if you open your heart to love, life will embrace you like a blanket of comfort on a cold winter night. Her spirit and essence will always be there with me!

One year has passed from the marked event of my daughter's passing. One fears to move on with life and struggles with the thought of ever forgetting her or better yet, truly letting go and living the next chapter of this book called "Life." I really believe, ***just like in every good book, the chapters before the one we are experiencing weave the very nature of the book itself, and therefore cannot be separated***. Without the previous chapters, there cannot be a book; there is no story. Such it is in life, our experiences (or better yet, individual vignettes) shape us (by integrating the sum of all the vignettes) to define a person's life. With this in mind, *it becomes clear that both joyfully experiencing the individual moments of the vignettes and processing in a healthy manner the sum of these vignettes, become the fundamental components associated with living a fruitful and productive life.*

Equally important is the ability of human beings to learn from the life experiences of others. As human beings, we can learn and try to model how exceptional people love and enjoy each moment or vignette being experienced. Most important, we can also learn how these exceptional human beings processed these individual vignettes into a fruitful and productive life. It is here where Krista's life, her experiences and essence of existence become a living example and testimony. If only I could intertwine Krista's ability to process life (individual vignettes and the sum of the vignettes) with my own being and nature. One thing is for sure: if I could ever accomplish this process, my life would become abundantly fruitful and richer. God willing, I will not give up hope. Just like in a book, sometimes the previous chapters are not being read now, but nevertheless, they are securely woven permanently within the book, and without them, the book would lack meaning and a sense of relevance.

I would like to think that Krista's spirit is in another dimension perfectly united and in peaceful coexistence with whatever entity or deity created this strange world. I firmly believe that she truly earned that right. I believe, that at times, we try to explain things in a spiritual sense to make us feel better about our existing conditions. In this case, I truly believe it is the only thing that makes logical sense. ***Krista's example of how to live, in my humble estimation, is clearly connected to a natural and non-forced evolution with the spiritual domain. Whatever was, is; and whatever is, will always be!***

In the final analysis, two things that we can control become clearly identified as the most important components of one's life:

- *To love*
- *To allow ourselves to be loved*

Krista masterfully grasped and conquered these two areas. Her life is a verifiable living example of how to live. Her life also offers, for those of us who want to see, permanent footprints for us to follow, entwined out of the marrow of perseverance and unconditional love.

Krista, may we remember your essence and legacy:

- To truly **live** each moment,
- To genuinely **love** the world around us,
- To joyfully **laugh** to make a difference,
- And to enjoy **life** to its fullest.

So, what are we to do when one gets struck with what appears to be an insurmountable blow! How do we persevere through the abyss when the blow and loss are so strong that you find yourself doubting the very value and meaning of existence? As I previously mentioned, love is the only antidote that life gives you to counter the void left behind. ***Love by its very nature creates a synergetic effect that manifests in what I call the language of God.*** *Love is the only way we can truly honor Krista's life, as she lived here on earth and wherever her spirit is breathing. I firmly believe that love is eternal and the only real and positive contribution we leave behind for humanity.*

Valuable Lessons Learned:

- *Just like in every good book, the chapters before the one we are experiencing weave the very nature of the book itself, and therefore cannot be separated.*
- *Krista's example of how to live, in my humble estimation, is clearly connected to a natural and non-forced evolution with the spiritual domain.*
- *In the final analysis two things that we can control become clearly identified as the most important components of one's life, to Love and allow ourselves to be Loved.*
- *Love by its very nature creates a synergetic effect that manifests in what I call the language of God.*

Chapter 11
Cause and Effect

For most of us, Disney World brings us back to our youth. We can even be childish there and no one will judge (or they shouldn't). It's the magic of Disney! Well, multiply that by one hundred when you're there with Krista-Marie. I am a child at heart, so going to Disney with Krista-Marie enlightened me and made me feel alive. I opened my heart and physically and emotionally placed myself in her world. My God, I felt so. . . free!

Oh me! Oh life! Of the questions of these recurring,
Of the endless trains of the faithless, of cities filled
    with the foolish,

Of myself forever reproaching myself, (for who more foolish than I, and who more faithless?)
Of eyes that vainly crave the light, of the objects mean, of the struggle ever renewed,
Of the poor results of all, of the plodding and sordid crowds I see around me,
Of the empty and useless years of the rest, with the rest me intertwined,
The question, O me! So sad, recurring—What good amid these, O me, O life?

Answer.

That you are here—that life exists and identity,
That the powerful play goes on, and you may contribute a verse

—Walt Whitman

I find this to be an extremely powerful statement, "That the powerful play goes on, and that you may contribute a verse." When paying close attention to what the writer is telling us in this verse, we discover the following:

- That the play or better yet, life itself, is already unfolding
- That inherent within the play, regardless of our action, is meaning
- That we don't have the power nor control to stop or pause the play
- That the play or life itself grants individuals the right to participate
- *That individuals have a choice in how they will contribute to the play, creating a cause and effect relationship uniquely dependent on the action (quality of the action or non-action taken) of the participant*

From my humble optic, life seems to unfold, as it should. **Certain laws of nature are constantly** *at work producing a variety of set responses. At times these set responses can produce positive results at the macro level, even if we as humans have a difficult time comprehending these laws of nature.* As an example, hurricanes are considered a horrible destroying force, especially for those people who lost loved ones or their homes as a result. However, storms, as well as hurricanes, serve to maintain the earth's heat balance. Hurricanes help to transfer heat away from the tropics. Furthermore, other storms serve to bring cold air to the tropics as well as carry warm air to the North and South Poles. It is hard to see the utility and purpose of these laws when you are personally affected.

It almost seems that humans imagine themselves to be miraculously outside the cause and effect of these natural laws. *From where I am standing, it sure seems that our ego and insecurities created and molded within our frame of mind obstruct the reality of the world around us.* How much control do we really have? As humans, we come into this world without much of a say and we exit it unable to alter the inevitable. Still, we erroneously believe that we can control, overpower, and influence the natural laws around us. There is beauty and sanity in accepting these natural laws. *There is freedom in connecting to a larger truth. This larger truth is constantly being displayed by the world around us. All we need to do is free ourselves from our mind or better yet, the unhealthy frames or set patterns created by our thoughts.*

There is a sense of order and balance when we connect ourselves to the present moment. The present moment is really all we have. Thoughts of our past and future can be helpful to connect to at times, but only if these thoughts produce a meaningful connection and outcome to the present moment. We can utilize thoughts pertaining to our past to learn and improve ourselves to live a more meaningful life in the present moment. Moreover, thoughts about the future can help us have meaningful goals for the present moment.

A family might decide that it would be wise as a future goal to be debt free, generating actions in the present moment of budgeting, spending less, and saving. The actions of the present moment—budgeting, spending less, and saving—impart the core of truth of the present moment and connect to the future goal wished for. If a future goal is not attached to the present moment, it is not grounded in reality or truth. *From my humble optic, any action not grounded in the reality or truth of the present moment can be detrimental to our wellbeing.*

Valuable Lessons Learned:

- *An individual has a choice in how they will contribute to the play, creating a cause and effect relationship uniquely dependent on the action (quality of the action or non-action taken) of the participant.*
- *Certain laws of nature are constantly at work producing a variety of set responses. At times these set responses can produce positive results at the macro level, even if we as humans have a difficult time comprehending these laws of nature.*
- *From where I am standing, it sure seems that our ego and insecurities created and molded within our frame of mind obstruct the reality of the world around us.*
- *There is freedom in connecting to a larger truth. This larger truth is constantly being displayed by the world around us. All we need to do is free ourselves from our mind or better yet, the unhealthy frames or set patterns created by our thoughts.*
- *From my humble optic, any action not grounded in the reality or truth of the present moment can be detrimental to our wellbeing.*

Chapter 12
The Philadelphia Trial

Bernie had a business conference to Philadelphia and asked me to join him. I went online and noticed that the conference had a Special Olympic 5K on a Sunday morning that he would probably have to meet with his staff. I took the initiative to play a proactive role and register for the 5K. Not ever participating in a 5K or even running was a part of my trials but separating from my family and participating in a city I had never been to nor did I know anyone there was, even more, a challenge. Well, time to take steps forward and jump into this! Luckily on the day of the race, Bernie was able to join me. At the start line, I saw the special-needs teenage boy excited and ready to run and lead us to the race. His energy was electrifying. I felt tears running down my cheeks as I looked at everyone uniting for this beautiful cause.

At that moment, it was like a lightning bolt had hit me emotionally. I realized that I had a purpose in life to make a difference with the love that was inside me. Equally important, I realized that inside myself existed the love that I was blessed with for twelve and a half years. This is the road to take. My life did not end. It is starting a new chapter. I need to take this baton and run with it for as long as I can and make a difference, and Krista-Marie will be by my side helping me through it. She is here and will always be part of me.

I injured myself during a charity run in Philadelphia. To my surprise, the injury was more severe than I imagined. I fractured my ankle and tore two ligaments. I was placed in an air boot and was told that the recovery would be slow due to the severity of the injury. Being a very active person, the reality of my present situation soon struck home.

Routinely, I have learned to exercise to alter my negative thoughts of past and future to the reality of the present moment. Through the years, it has become second nature to generate this action producing healthy outcomes. The injury caused an abrupt change in my lifestyle, especially not being able to exercise in order to alter my thoughts. As months passed, ***it became clear that my present reality had become different.*** I no longer could exercise to ground myself to the reality of the moment. When I studied myself, I experienced that my mind was now generating an unhealthy pattern of thoughts that primarily focused on the past and future. The following pattern of thoughts are listed as an example:

- I can't believe that four months have passed, and I still can't walk. I might never be able to walk or exercise the way I used to.
- Why did I have to do the charity run? How stupid! Why did not I walk the charity event instead of running?
- If I can't walk soon, my job might be affected.
- If my job is affected, my family's lifestyle will dramatically change.
- Life continues at another pace, while I sit and can't engage at the level that I want.

I quickly realized that these thoughts were creating a change in my moods and behavior. What made it worse was that I could no longer use the instrument (exercise) used in the past to alter my unhealthy thought patterns. *I needed to ground myself in the reality of my current situation. I also needed to allow and come to terms with my emotions of the present moment.* It was fine to be frustrated or sad; what had to change were the thought patterns of the past and future framing a final outcome. From my view, *the only reality was the present moment, shaped by present emotions and feelings accompanying them*. Within that context, I needed to open myself to see the very real events occurring all around me. My injury, as painful and frustrating as it was, was not the only important incident occurring. *I needed to remove my focus on myself in order to see the reality happening all around me.*

The truth is that I was not participating in the Philadelphia Charity 5K event for myself. Unknowingly, the Philadelphia charity event represented a major step in my wife's (Marta) healing process. The event created a path for Marta to find purpose in a new chapter of her life. Sometimes, when we focus on our own apparent crucible, we might miss the great value and positive effect the experience and process might be representing for others. Although my injuries were an unpleasant experience, I would gladly do it all over again!

Valuable Lessons Learned:

- *It became clear that my present reality had become different.*
- *I needed to ground myself in the reality of my current situation. I also needed to allow and come to terms with my emotions of the present moment.*
- *The only reality is the present moment, shaped by present emotions and feelings accompanying them.*
- *I needed to remove the focus from myself in order to see the reality happening all around me.*

Chapter 13
Connecting Rods of the Past, Present, and Future

A kiss goodnight! Krista-Marie had a beautiful stress-free routine every night prior to bedtime. Krista-Marie's routine was as follows: a calm bath, PJs, two Fig Newtons, yogurt, puzzle, Bumblebee educational DVD, and a kiss goodnight. I felt a bond, a feeling that I was making a lasting memory.

I firmly believe that ***past events are connected producing a cause and effect scenario,*** *which depending on the participant's level of awareness regarding this relationship (cause and effect) can produce an altering outcome of the present moment.* We can greatly benefit if we learn and examine this reality. An example of this can be seen in sports. Let's assume that a top athlete has not trained as adequately as he should have for a big race. Let's also contemplate that the athlete just came back from nursing a hamstring injury. On the day of the race the athlete will ask his body, including his hamstring, to produce at a maximum effort. When his body is asked to produce at maximum force, the weakest area of the body fails, and the athlete receives another tear to his hamstring.

In this example, the past actions (lack of training and weak hamstring) are clearly connected to the present moment (big race). The past actions of the athlete influenced the outcome of the present moment (the athlete reinjured himself). Equally displayed in this example is that the past clearly influenced the present moment when connected to the same sphere or field of activity. If the athlete had received an injury to his finger and had not used his injured finger for a month, the degree of influence to the present moment (in this example the athlete reinjuring himself) would have been different. This can be attributed to the injury to the finger (past event) not having an altering connection to the event or race (present moment).

It is my belief that in the same fashion future events are also connected to this sphere or range of field activity, fusing the future to the past and present. *The future must connect to some event from the past and present sphere in order to exist.*

Once we understand clearly that the present moment is influenced by events from the past that are connected to a range of field activity, then we can alter or modify the final outcome in the present moment just before it transforms into our future. Using the example of our athlete, if the athlete would have identified these connecting rods from the past, present, and future, he could have altered his future outcome by generating a different course of action in the present moment. The athlete could have altered his future path and injury by doing the following:

- Not participating in the event when realizing he had not trained or rehabilitated his hamstring adequately
- Time permitting, dedicated maximum effort to training and rehabilitation, nursing the injured hamstring to a satisfactory or optimum level

I also humbly believe that this same situation (the present moment being influenced by events from the past if connected to a range of field activity) occurs at a much deeper level if we allow ourselves to see it. In the example of the athlete, the athlete can only change the final outcome if he sees the connecting rods from the past and present and chooses to take another course of action, therefore changing the inevitable future.

If this holds true in the example given of the athlete, would it hold true for other more eventful situations? My daughter Krista is no longer physically with us, but at a much deeper level our (mine and Krista's) past, present, and future, if grasped genuinely, are connected. ***Krista's nature and essence are as true today as they were when she was living on this earth. This essence and nature were and are interconnected to my past, and if I am willing to understand it at a deeper level, also can be interconnected to my present.*** As an example, Krista's consistent natural and effortless way of loving is an illustration of an area we can connect to. It is important to note that what I am describing is more than just connecting to a past experience or love that I experienced from her when she was alive. ***The past helps me to value the truth of her essence. In this case, the way she loved.*** If I had not experienced her truth it would have been difficult to validate it as being part of her essence. Once this has been achieved (connecting to the reality of her essence through the window of the past) we must continue to examine the experience at a much deeper level. Physics informs us that energy is never lost and that the electrical energy radiated by our brain does not vanish from existence. It recycles as other unknown forms of energy. I humbly suggest for us to consider the following:

- If love exists as a field of energy, and if energy as the laws of physics inform us is never lost but recycled as other forms of energy, then can it be also true that following the same energy conversion, Krista's love or energy has been transformed into another field of energy or better yet, maybe immersed deep within us. *Can it also be true that Krista as an energy force herself has converted into another and purer form of energy possibly in another dimension that we don't understand or remotely master?* Is the resurrection an energy conversion into another dimension? If this turns out to be true, then wouldn't it make sense that our energy conversion would transform itself into a pure and unaltered perfect love? From where I am standing, I can see no better definition of heaven. Could it be possible for Krista to communicate this love, in a different fashion, from her present state or condition? Can we learn to harness this energy or love radiated by her in our present moment or state of being? It is this faith, hope, and love that provides a sense of peace for family members that have lost a loved one.

- From my humble optic, the only way I see possible to do this is for us to be able to radiate a similar wavelength of energy that matches or is similar to the one that she (Krista) is conveying, and furthermore to be receptive to see and receive the love or energy being radiated back to us within our sphere of existence. One can only hope that such a thing is true and possible. Analyzing this position from my knowledge and experiences, I cannot imagine a heaven more perfect than this: a transformation into a perfect and unaltered state of love. For me having the fortune of having experienced a magnitude of unconditional love from Krista when she was on this earth and being keenly aware of how love is of utmost importance for us as a species, I can see no other transformation but this one!

Valuable Lessons Learned:

- *Past events are connected producing a cause and effect scenario, which depending on the participant's level of awareness regarding this relationship (cause and effect) can produce an altering outcome of the present moment.*
- *The future must connect to some event from the past and present sphere in order to exist.*
- *Krista's essence and nature were and are interconnected to my past, and if I am willing to understand it at a deeper level, are also interconnected in my present and future.*
- *The past helps me to value the truth of her essence. In this case, the way she loved.*
- *Can it also be true that Krista as an energy force herself has converted into another and purer form of energy possibly in another dimension that we don't understand or remotely master?*

Chapter 14
A Pillar of Strength

Acknowledging that Krista-Marie might not reach certain goals in her life was a rude awakening. However, once you allow your mind not to be locked, you start to step out of the box and allow your creative mind to plan a different future, a future with other possibilities and unseen potentials. We first set ourselves up financially and legally so that both girls would be protected in case something happened to us. Then, we started planning our lives centered on our family priorities and disconnected from unneeded excesses. It's incredible how your frame of mind can be your best friend when you are looking at life with a different perspective. We don't always have control of life, but we do have to accept, let go, be thankful, and manage how life unfolds.

I find that my wife embodies some of the same genuine character traits that Krista possessed. Marta has a natural disposition to be kindhearted and considerate to the individuals she meets. Recently, we completed a personality test to enquire which were our highest-rated individual personality traits. Marta's top two personality traits were *conscientious* ("A tendency to be organized and dependable, show self-discipline, act dutifully, aim for achievement, and prefer planned rather than spontaneous behavior") and *devoted*. It is interesting to point out that a person possessing the trait of being devoted has a natural disposition for the following:

1. Seeking out others' opinions when making decisions; following others' advice
2. Promoting good feelings between yourself and the important people in your life; promoting harmony; being polite, agreeable, and tactful
3. Being thoughtful of others, and being good at pleasing them; enduring personal discomfort to do a good turn for the key people in your life
4. Being thoroughly dedicated to the relationships in your life; placing the highest value on sustained relationships; respecting the institution of marriage and avowals of commitment; working hard to keep your relationships going

I sometimes wondered how my wife endured the hardships and sacrifices allotted to her. As previously mentioned, there is a common belief that a person will naturally adjust and sustain the hardships allotted to them proportionally to their own survival. I have personally seen this common belief disproved numerous times, as for some individuals the fear and horror being faced becomes too unbearable to overcome. In some cases, even if the hardships are surmounted, the wounds left behind alter one's perception of the very essence of life.

I have seen on many occasions, devastating personality changes in human beings unable to psychologically process or manage the storms of life. I find this to be especially true when the storms of life arrive one after another, with little room to rest or navigate a manageable solution.

The same is equally true when one storm is so severe that it tears down the very fabric of existence. When this occurs, a person is faced with the inability to alter events due to the state of permanency of the hardship being faced (death of a loved one, etc.). Based on this situation, a person is left with the following choices:

- Not accepting the outcome, staying firmly rooted in the past, and ignoring the present outcome. This choice has a grinding effect on individuals as the natural process of life is continuously rooted in the present moment.
- Accepting the outcome but being unable to redefine one's life within the present moment. This choice inhibits growth and erodes the love

and zest for life, due to our fear of truly letting go of the past, our inability to release emotionally the terror felt, or the possibility of facing similar blows in the future.

- *Accepting the outcome to the point of redefining one's life within the present moment. This choice once accepted and processed, although the most difficult one to travel, provides an individual with a sense of purpose and hope within the present.* This choice, when processed correctly, redefines the current relationship of the loved one that has passed away within the context of present reality. One's faith, according to everyone's belief system, can sustain a very real, personal, and present-moment relationship with the loved one that passed away.

As a child, my wife endured several difficult hardships. Her mother, who herself was disowned at the age of nine and raised by her aunt, suffered from severe insecurities created by these experiences. It is reasonable to believe that these insecurities could have influenced her parenting abilities. To say the least, this had an impact on Marta's relationship. However strenuous, these difficulties taught my wife how to fight and survive, and above all, build a strong sense of self, influenced by several key figures:

- Her father (an unconditionally loving man who was the person Marta relied on for emotional and day-to-day support)
- Her great aunt (gave her a sense of value for who she was as a person and taught her the meaning of self-respect)

Just as in Krista's case, Marta also possessed and possesses unique and innate God-given abilities. These abilities allowed her to navigate and transform extremely difficult situations into the very building blocks needed to foster within her personality such important traits as integrity, honesty, and most importantly an open and loving heart.

Marta grew up strong and with a sense of independence, always seeking comfort from the positive influences in her life. Equally important, she remained psychologically distant to the people imparting negative energy. This ability to seek comfort around positive influences and at the same time repel negativity proved vital for her survival and sanity. Furthermore, it provided healthy habits that are still deeply embedded within her essence. Marta commenced very early in her youth to radiate love to those around her. ***This ability to constantly love and serve the people around her has proven to be one of Marta's greatest strengths and has served as the very antidote to combat her trials and tribulations.***

But like I always say, God works within imperfect situations to shape perfection. Marta's genetic code and God-given personality were the key ingredients not only to minimize the adverse effect of negative situations but also to create the necessary experiences to strengthen and further develop her for the trials she would face in the future. Marta developed a rare combination of strengths that when mixed together became one powerful concoction. She became an extremely kind and loving human being, with an unimaginable source of strength to endure difficult situations.

Throughout the years, my wife also developed the art of focusing and grounding herself on the positive side of events while staying far from the reach of negative emotions and destructive outcomes. It is clear to me that both of my daughters, Katrina and Krista, were awarded the perfect mother to shape their world and development.

Marta became very successful in the healthcare industry and throughout her career became the manager of several healthcare companies. A memorable decision for our family occurred when my first-born, Katrina, was going to start first grade. Marta was earning more money than me at the time, but the realization that Katrina would need to be placed in an aftercare program due to our work schedules became an agonizing thought. Marta looked at me and calmly stated that one of us had to leave their employment to take care of Katrina. She then added that the person should be her due to my job providing more stability and a pension.

Marta left an annual salary of over $160,000 on the table. There was no severance package, so the financial adjustment was from earning a salary to no income. She left her career identity and replaced it with an absolute dedication and care to Katrina and our family. Although the financial burden was rough, it was the best decision we ever made as a family. One of Marta's true gifts is her ability to prioritize the things in life that are the most valuable. It is amazing how someone can be so grounded in the very essence and true worth of existence. There was no complaint or hesitation. Marta's decision proved monumental for our family. Her and Katrina became inseparable, and together they were able to enjoy school functions, ballet, volleyball, swimming, and a host of additional recreational and academic activities. Katrina's development and security would be radically transformed and shaped by a family's ability to see what is truly important. The Greeks called the love of *agape* (unconditional love) the most powerful of the loves. It is amazing how something written thousands of years ago can still be so true today.

The value of Marta's decision became pronounced with the birth of Krista. Due to Krista's learning disabilities, the family had to adapt to different roles and responsibilities. Therapies (both at home and away), hyperbaric oxygen sessions, and medical procedures would become everyday events for our family. I still recall Marta having to go inside the hyperbaric chamber with Krista to calm her fears. One of the things I admire the most about my wife is that through all of Krista's therapies, difficult sessions, and medical procedures, she still was very aware of Katrina's development and emotional security. I can clearly recall while Krista was still a baby, Marta stating that Katrina had to be equally protected so she could live the carefree life of a teenager. Our family's way of life would integrate these two philosophies:

1. Grounded in love, do whatever humanly possible to allow Katrina to enjoy her childhood and teen years as carefree as possible
2. Grounded in love, show Katrina that her sister had special needs needing individual dedication and care from the family

Looking back at our situation, I would strongly suggest that any family going through similar struggles to consider the integration of these two philosophies. Although life unfolded some difficult situations and hardships along the way, from my humble optic, there was considerable wisdom and benefit to our family by following this way of life.

Valuable Lessons Learned:

- *The same is equally true when one storm is so severe that it tears down the very fabric of existence. When this occurs, a person is faced with the inability to alter events due to the state of permanency of the hardship being faced (death of a loved one, etc.).*
- *Accepting the outcome to the point of redefining one's life within the present moment. (This choice, once accepted and processed, although the most difficult one to travel, provides an individual with a sense of purpose and hope within the present.)*
- *This ability to constantly love and serve the people around her has proven to be one of Marta's greatest strengths and has served as the very antidote to combat her trials and tribulations.*

Chapter 15
A Portrait of Courage

My first daughter, Katrina's, eyes were so excited to meet her sister, Krista. Through a glass window, she looked intently and pointed at her sister with excitement. What a wonderful memory! Katrina, our first daughter, was born on June 10, 1992, months before Hurricane Andrew ripped through South Florida, deeply affecting the welfare of families in the Miami and Broward County areas. I was working on a special mission with the police department helping the hundreds of police personnel and families left without shelter and essentials. I was working a twelve hours on/twelve hours off schedule without days off for close to a year. Our townhouse, although damaged by the storm, was still standing and provided shelter for Marta and Katrina. Marta concentrated on parenting Katrina and helped the police officers in need however she could. On one occasion, a husband and wife that had lost everything in the storm slept the night in our townhouse. Marta fed them breakfast, lunch, and dinner, providing the only hot meal they had received in weeks. I enjoyed my family enormously during my few hours at home. It is amazing how much you miss your family when situations force you to be away from them. I guess you could say it is fitting that ***Katrina was born into changing times, and without her knowledge life was training Katrina to assume the lessons she would have to endure.***

Katrina grew up a happy and well-balanced child, being the center of the universe for Marta and me. Trips to Disney, Key Largo, Marco Island, and Sarasota, were a familiar routine for our family. A familiar routine was also my dad, mom, and niece and nephew traveling with our family everywhere we went. It was a happy and rewarding time for our family, a time that every member will always value immensely. As mentioned earlier, Marta left her job to concentrate more on Katrina's wellbeing. Marta and Katrina were tied at the hip since birth, making a strong bond that would be tested in the future. Katrina was so close to Marta that my mom once told her (Marta) that she was very concerned that their level of closeness could affect Katrina if something traumatic happened to her. My mom believed that Katrina would be unable to deal with the separation if something happened to Marta. Although, thank God, Katrina did not have to endure Marta passing, she did have to endure her sister's disability and passing.

Katrina had to adjust to difficult situations that our family encountered. During her sister's birth, she was unable to see her because Krista was in intensive care. As mentioned earlier, we did not know if Krista was going to live, and the doctor believed she had spinal meningitis. *Imagine a parent having to figure out what to say to his/her eight-year-old daughter about what was happening to her sister. There is no manual or parenting guidebook for situations like this. Thus, a parent must rely on their spiritual instinct, an instinct that gradually reveals a deep awareness and knowledge of the essence of their child.*

Although Marta and I worked extremely hard for Katrina to have a normal (personally, I hate the word *normal*) childhood, it was impossible for Katrina to ignore and discount the countless therapy sessions and doctors' visits her sister was subjected to. *In the end, Katrina tried to adjust and be supportive, but as a child, she was caught between a perception of the world she wanted to live in (the world she had before her sister was born) and the very real awareness of her sister needing help and support.* This situation became more complex as Katrina became a teenager and faced the hormonal changes associated with her age. Katrina's courage to endure and do her best is nothing short of remarkable. I remember Marta constantly telling me that Katrina should talk to someone to help her deal with her sister's condition. I believe Marta was right and it was an error on my part not to support this. From my optic, a family pulls together and supports the member needing the most help. I grew up with this philosophy and mantra, and at the time never saw the need for Katrina seeing someone to talk to. Katrina participated in ballet recitals and volleyball and had a nucleus of friends that stayed together throughout elementary, middle, and high school.

Katrina developed a special and unique bond with her sister. When they had disagreements and Krista tried to take away Katrina's food, stuffed animals, etc., she would tell her sister no and proceed to tell us that this was her way of having a healthy relationship with her sibling. She strongly believed that it was healthy for her to have the normal sister squabbles like any other sister, regardless of what other hardships Krista was enduring. This attitude was very wise and helped to support their relationship and friendship.

When it came close to time for Katrina to graduate from high school, Marta and I thought Katrina would be going away to Central Florida with one of her close friends. One day, over lunch, in what was then her favorite restaurant, I asked her about her thoughts of going away to college. I also mentioned that her sister was not her responsibility and she had a right to choose to go with her friend and enjoy the college experience. Katrina had earned a full scholarship and had prepaid college, so there was no financial burden for the family. Katrina informed me that she was very comfortable living at home and believed she needed to support us with Krista. She told us that it was her decision to stay.

Katrina did not know at the time that her decision would positively impact her life forever, for it would help her develop an even stronger relationship with her sister. One can only imagine the possible adverse effect her sister's passing would have had on her if she had decided to go away to college. Katrina's essence, love for the family, and closeness and special relationship with every member of our family provided the strength to make such a decision. I respect, honor, and love my daughter Katrina dearly!

Valuable Lessons Learned:

- *Katrina was born into changing times, and without her knowledge, life was training Katrina to assume the lessons she would have to endure.*
- *Imagine a parent having to figure out what to say to his/her eight-year-old daughter about what was happening to her sister. There is no manual or parenting guidebook for situations like this. Thus, a parent must rely on their spiritual instinct, an instinct that gradually reveals a deep awareness and knowledge of the essence of their child.*
- *In the end, Katrina tried to adjust and be supportive, but as a child, she was caught between a perception of the world she wanted to live in (the world she had before her sister was born) and the very real awareness of her sister needing help and support.*

Chapter 16
Agape

I still remember how I would dance with Krista in the pool. I would hold her so gently and move with the music, all the while Krista feeling the music within the deepest fiber of her soul. I would also sing and play out the meaning of the music, as Krista took every ounce of emotion and intention deep within. I believe some souls possess the gift to feel the music as a conduit to feed the soul. Krista-Marie and I shared this gift!

As so wisely stated, you don't receive a manual that dictates all the proper steps to be followed when you raise your family. But one thing that *our Creator did provide for us is the perfect antidote to parental mishaps. As previously mentioned, this antidote is thoroughly rooted in the spirit of unconditional love. As I see it, unconditional love is the act of consistently radiating loving energy or loving actions on someone else.*

The antithesis of unconditional love is an unbalanced ego, consistently generating energy and actions that only point in your direction and in line with your own desires. One can see how misfortunate it would be for a family, especially one with a member needing special attention, to take the mantra of selfish love as a philosophy. *The manifestation of this action would be monumental for every person of the family, including the family member manifesting the selfish love.* It is important to note that every person has their own unique genetic coding and personality making them naturally more or less selfish. What is important to grasp is that as a family, we, according to our genetic code, were doing the best we could adhering to this philosophy or way of life.

The Book of the Tao, Analects of Confucius, Buddhism, and the teachings of Christ all point to a natural process of accepting the trials and tribulations of this life. Christ speaks of not fretting or excessively agonizing over the things we do not have control over and to accept the conditions life brings to us by a process of shifting our worries and anxieties toward the direction and control of our Creator.

Oriental writings teach us to read the streams of life with a sense of awareness and acceptance, never traveling opposite to the indicated direction. Traveling opposite stream will simply increase pain and suffering. The continuation of traveling in the opposite stream will eventually lead to our inner and outer destruction.

Although I firmly believe what I have written to be true, the accepting of one's lot and moving forward within the new streams of life is quite challenging and extremely difficult. ***It appears that the mind takes comfort and security in the known and resists the notion of moving in the direction of a new stream of life.*** This condition is marked when an individual loses a loved one that represented a major part of their life. When this occurs, the mind fights hard to remain locked with the loved one's memories creating all sorts of complications and guilt when the individual attempts to move in the direction of the newly directed stream.

The death of our daughter Krista was an extremely hard blow for every member of my family. Marta's ability to persevere and move forward during these times represents an inner strength that I have only seen once before in my life (in my father). She balanced keeping the integrity of Krista's essence and memory with the difficult task of moving forward toward a new direction in her life. She did this by allowing herself to grieve naturally, an important point to grasp for anyone going through a loss of a close friend or family member. ***There is no secret to the grieving process, except allowing it to flow naturally and effortlessly.***

One can analyze and logically deduce the correct steps to take without allowing the natural and emotional healing process to occur. The byproduct of not allowing this natural emotional healing process to occur is the manifestation of all kinds of mental and physical illnesses. I am very fortunate to have Marta as my wife, partner, and friend! Her unconditional love and constant acts of kindness have made me a better person and have provided a breath of hope during some very difficult times.

Valuable Lessons Learned:

- *One thing our Creator did provide for us is the perfect antidote to parental mishaps. As previously mentioned, this antidote is thoroughly rooted in the spirit of unconditional love. As I see it, unconditional love is the act of consistently radiating loving energy or loving actions on someone else.*
- *It appears that the mind takes comfort and security in the known and resists the notion of moving in the direction of a new stream of life.*
- *The antithesis of unconditional love is an unbalanced ego, consistently generating energy and actions that only point in your direction and in line with your own desires.*
- *There is no secret to the grieving process, except allowing it to flow naturally and effortlessly.*

Chapter 17
A Touch of Love

As a family with a young daughter, we felt we needed to explore a calm family beach, and that's how we discovered Marco Island. Not as clear as the Atlantic, but it offered little to no waves and a certain serenity that was priceless. As the years went by, Marco Island and Walt Disney World became the two hot spots for our family. How did we budget and when could we go? We budgeted and we went as much as we could. Why not, it's heaven! Naturally, Bernie's parents and his niece and nephew were always attached to our hips. We had countless trips together. When Krista-Marie came into our lives, this became her perfect beach and second home. The beach is a natural stimulant. It's an abundance of senses that combined with family creates the best memories some families can possibly have. Collecting seashells and matching the colors intrigued Krista-Marie's curiosity and made this an activity that I will forever cherish. There's nothing like looking at your daughter's beautiful image by the seashore sitting on a lounge chair enjoying an afternoon snack as she observes her family engaging or watching me attempt to fly a Disney Princess kite. Krista-Marie did not do well with too much sun exposure but enjoyed early morning and late afternoon walks on the beach followed by family cookouts and the laughter of a family that embraces the definition of love as a bond that will last forever. Marco Island is still a haven for us. A Disney Princess kite is flown every year on Krista-Marie's birthday, and we still collect shells together. It is where Krista-Marie will forever be... free with no limitations.

Marta envisioned opening a non-profit charity organization to honor Krista's name and legacy. The idea was a way to celebrate the way Krista lived, a method to connect to her essence and radiate her love toward others. The vision was to collect funds in her name and provide these funds to the actual schools and therapy centers helping children diagnosed with autism learning disabilities. I am sure that Krista's spirit favors this idea due to the resources impacting the children directly. Opening a non-profit charity organization is not an easy venture, especially when you are totally ignorant of the legalities and paperwork needed. *I am certain that love guided the way and through its share of perseverance, the non-profit organization was opened.* The name we came up with, Krista-Marie Touch of Love, was a very appropriate name considering we wanted to radiate Krista's essence and love. *The non-profit charity's mission and overarching goal was to produce a positive effect in the lives of children with learning disabilities.*

Another primary goal was to help the parents of these children that might be overwhelmed with their existing situation. With the help of many wonderful people, our first two events have been a great success. Whole Food donated 5 percent of their earnings on St. Patrick's Day in Krista's name. We collected over $4,000 dollars. The second event was a $5,000 race held on Krista's Birthday (April 12). We signed up more than 180 people, who, bless their hearts, woke up at 5:00 a.m. to participate. It is important to note that teachers, therapists, principals, and family members impacted by Krista's essence participated as well as perfect strangers who were pleasantly surprised to learn the reason that they were running for.

Suffice it to say that Krista's spirit was present and the love that was displayed by everyone participating was as close as one can get to the essence of God and its spiritual presence within each of us if we only bother to see and welcome it.

Valuable Lessons Learned:

- *I am certain that love guided the way and through its share of perseverance the non-profit organization was opened.*
- *The non-profit charity's mission and overarching goal was to produce a positive effect in the lives of children with learning disabilities.*
- *Suffice it to say that Krista's spirit was present, and the love that was displayed by everyone participating was as close as one can get to the essence of God and its spiritual presence within each of us if we only bother to see and welcome it.*

Chapter 18
Silent Heroes

One day I was so enraged because they were going to leave Krista with her current teacher and not advance her to the next level. I still remember how I corralled Ms. Safe (school principal) and let go of all my emotions on this wonderful lady. Shortly after, I realized that Ms. Safe's assessment was correct and apologized to her profusely. What is important to recognize is Ms. Safe's emotional intelligence and ability to allow a father's frustrations to come out. What level of wisdom!

From that day on I became Ms. Safe's champion and trusted her implicitly.

There is always a short list of what I call *silent heroes*, in everyone's life. **These silent heroes can sometimes be instrumental to our wellbeing and existence. They can sometimes represent the very pillars that support your very essence.** In Krista's case, there were many individuals that helped through countless medical procedures and therapy sessions. As a parent one is extremely thankful for the support this group of individuals offered. They are a special group of individuals, or silent heroes, that represented so much more to my daughter. They represented security, unconditional love, and a level of friendship that is seldom seen in this world. Krista unconditionally loved and was a genuine friend to this group of individuals. Krista's unconditional actions would not have surprised anyone that knew my daughter. Krista received unconditional love and genuine friendship from these silent heroes, making it possible for her to have a sense of security and emotional intelligence rarely seen in conventional children and adults.

There are two schools that need to be mentioned, as these unsung heroes belong to these institutions. Two very special people lead Panther Run Elementary and Angel's Reach. Mrs. Safe and Mrs. Luzado are transcendental organizational leaders in one of the most important fields in life:

the safeguarding of our children's future. Mrs. Safe is the principal of Panther Run Elementary.

Krista was very fortunate to encounter some exceptional human beings in Panther Run Elementary School that poured their love and time unconditionally for her benefit and wellbeing. As previously mentioned, there was also a symbiotic relationship among this group of individuals and Krista that produced a kind of unconditional love seldom witnessed in a school setting or life in general. One can only marvel and be humbly grateful having witnessed this kind of special moment. As parents, we are eternally grateful for the love displayed by these special people.

Sometimes in parenting, it seems that every door is closing and the efforts to help your child fall aimlessly without any fruit. It was while facing one of these moments that we met Mrs. Dory Luzado. At the time, we did not have a place for Krista's therapies that we felt comfortable as parents. Another complication was that our insurance would only cover a few therapies. As parents and teachers of the learning disabled can relate, therapies represent the only hope families have to make it through the dark skies. Dory opened her heart and center and offered an array of therapies both at home and at Angel's Reach. *The formula that worked for my daughter was excellent-quality therapies coupled with a genuine love from the therapists. This love was received by Krista and reciprocated by her toward the therapists in unimaginable quantities. This exchange, when allowed to flow naturally, can be the tipping point that produces a kind of love that alters one's existence.*

The only thing in life that I know that can truly alter one's spiritual existence in a positive dimension is the power of unconditional love. Through the many years at Angel's Reach, Krista benefited and developed as a happy and loving child. Words can never explain with any type of merit the void they helped fill in our lives.

Valuable Lessons Learned:

- *These silent heroes can sometimes be instrumental to our wellbeing and existence. They can sometimes represent the very pillars that support your very essence.*
- *The formula that worked for my daughter was excellent-quality therapies coupled with a genuine love from the therapists. This love was received by Krista and reciprocated by her toward the therapists in unimaginable quantities.*
- *This exchange, when allowed to flow naturally, can be the tipping point that produces a kind of love that alters one's existence.*

Chapter 19
Real Self-Worth

I remember coming stressed from a long day at work. I would silently come into the house and go straight to Krista's room for therapy. Krista would get on my back and massage my back with her elbows. These therapy sessions worked miracles to release my pent-up stress!

When examining the following quotations, "Where does the power come from to see the race to its end? It comes from within," from Eric Liddell, and "The enemy is within the gates; it is with our own luxury, our own folly, our own criminality that we have to contend," from Marcus Tullius Cicero, it is apparent that as human beings the power to be positive and constructive or negative and destructive about our situations comes from within.

It is my theory that we come to this world uniquely crafted in personality and spirit. If this is true, the more we allow ourselves to connect to this unique design shaped for our well-being, the more we can make sense of our situations and events. Moreover, if this statement is valid, then the inverse may also be true: the more we pull away from this unique design, the more confused, stressed, and distorted the content of our situations.

What occurs in life is that we block and distort this unique and specifically designed essence with our life baggage; the life baggage that we hold onto or repress pollutes and clogs our true being. Once it's clogged enough, everything, even our essence, is distorted! A simple example might clarify my theory.

A mother raising her first child commences the difficult task of parenting. She pulls from and is supported by her own childrearing experiences to raise her newly born child. As accustomed to in her upbringing, she commences putting a value on education. She remembers that she was a straight-A student throughout high school and college. Unbeknownst to the mother, the unique design and makeup of her daughter is different, and the child commences to struggle with some of the educational material as she enters middle school. The mother, not understanding these differences, creates and exerts pressure to support the value believed important (education). The child tries and tries but can never reach her mother's expectation.

Because of this, the child commences enhancing the character trait of perseverance, mainly to acquire a sense of value from her mother. Unfortunately, the child also begins to believe that she is unintelligent and unable to please her mother or match her intelligence. As this untruth is believed and attaches firmly to her mind and subconscious, the child becomes insecure not only in this area (education) but in other areas as well, due to the errant belief that she is unable to please her mother. As these insecurities manifest, they choke the joy and independent essence of the child's life, as the child's only wish is to be valued by her mom. Regrettably, this situation continues as the child develops into adulthood, creating all sorts of insecurities and distortions within her inner self.

Although we can attest to many situations of the example above, I firmly believe that individuals can liberate themselves from this level of hurt and thinking by acknowledging and coming to terms with their true self-worth. This true self-worth is not connected to a parent's value but is manifested in the very essence of being. Our Creator, spiritual essence, and life itself provide us with an inherent value that can't be removed by anyone. It just is! However, we can choose to ignore this truth and believe that our sense of value comes from pleasing or getting the validation of others (parents, husband/wife, friends, etc.).

I firmly believe that my daughter Krista understood this truth in the most genuine and natural fashion. Her true value never came into question because it radiated from within! I agree that our genetic makeup, upbringing, and experiences can have monumental effects that at times can severely handicap us, but *in the end, although difficult to accomplish, we have the choice not to believe our inner thoughts or existing frame of mind, therefore liberating us from becoming hostage to what we have been told or taught or have experienced.* We have the choice to grasp, accept, and believe our God-given true value and essence. By doing this we slowly create new thoughts and frames of mind that are naturally integrated with our intrinsic essence. As a student of life, I am still learning to fully grasp this undeniable truth, a truth that my daughter Krista naturally grasped from birth!

Valuable Lessons Learned:

- *What occurs in life is that we block and distort this unique and specifically designed essence with our life baggage; the life baggage that we hold onto or repress pollutes and clogs our true being. Once it's clogged enough, everything, even our essence, is distorted.*
- *I firmly believe that my daughter Krista understood this truth in the most genuine and natural fashion. Her true value never came into question because it radiated from within.*
- *In the end, although difficult to accomplish, we have the choice not to believe our inner thoughts or existing frame of mind, therefore liberating us from becoming hostage to what we have been told or taught or have experienced.*

Chapter 20
Control and Identity

Krista-Marie had a way of winning people's hearts during therapy and school. She was cute, adorable, and gave the best hugs. They really were the best!

This story is about Ryan. Ryan was a young man that worked at Krista-Marie's Panther Run Elementary School as a teacher's aide alongside with an incredible teacher called Mrs. Garrison. During the school year, Ryan's mother was struggling with cancer. Ryan had no dad or siblings to assist his mother with the everyday struggles and challenges that came with this incredible responsibility.

Ryan would break down sometimes and tell me that he was so scared to lose his mom. He loved his mom dearly, and she'd sacrificed her entire life for him.

Mrs. Garrison would share with me, "How will he get through this?"

At the end of the day, Ryan would walk out with Krista-Marie and smile and tell me all the wonderful things Krista-Marie had done throughout the day.

"Mrs. Gonzalez, Krista-Marie is amazing. Today, she did this…"

Ryan would smile and then tell me, "Mrs. Gonzalez, I'm so scared, but when Krista-Marie laughs and smiles, I'm so distracted. She helps me get through the day." When Krista-Marie passed away, we dedicated the Tree of Life to Panther Run Elementary School. It stands tall alongside a bench in their garden area.

The Tree of Life blooms beautiful pink flowers. It is a symbol of strength and beauty in our community that all children, regardless of their disabilities, should have the potential to grow up strong and beautiful and have every opportunity to reach their full potential in life.

Ryan continued looking for comfort by praying by the Tree of Life during his mom's last days. He explained to me that he never felt alone when he sat by the tree. Both Ryan and Mrs. Garrison are still part of our lives.

The tides of life bring some unexpected events that clearly unravel the notion of having control. This feeling of not having control can be accentuated by life offering a series of consecutive blows or if a traumatic event is connected somehow with a past unpleasant event. When we find ourselves in these kinds of situations, the brain fights and reacts to escape the pain being felt, especially if it is connected somehow to an impactful past event. At times our thoughts and created frames of minds can create obstacles to healing and healthy living. **Sometimes our** *consciousness can be extremely clear on what to do, but our emotions are the ones lagging needing a forum of expression.* Without a healthy balance of the two, there can't be healthy growth and development. Add to this personality differences that can sometimes complicate matters even further. This, in turn, can generate very unpleasant cause and effect reactions to our existence.

Our emotions escape the pain to survive, creating a distortion of thinking in order to feel secure and safe with the hope of altering the possibility of life causing another blow. Your emotions can even manifest all kinds of illnesses (real and self-generated) with the hope of avoiding or altering another traumatic event. While this is happening, our consciousness is fully aware of the futility of what is occurring. ***The fight for control is futile and nonexistent.*** Hardships and unfolding events will continue to occur, regardless of how much we try to control or escape.

This reminds me of Whitman's poem (mentioned earlier, but worth repeating) where he describes the hardships, sufferings, and difficulties of life, and in an act of desperation asks, "What is the meaning of life?" The answer comes back from God (as I interpret it) that you are *alive* and have an *identity*, that the powerful play must *go on* and you have been granted the gift of *playing a part* in it. ***There is incredible value in being alive and in***

having an individual identity with the freedom to create and choose our actions and attitudes. It is also important to realize, although at times very painful to grasp, the incredible truth and value associated with life moving on and evolving. Moreover, the fact that we are invited to play a part is an incredible gift that should be cherished. We have a choice as to the kind of chapter we write in the book of life. Will the contents of our chapter describe our lives from the perspective of fear, insecurity, untruth, pain, anger, and a state of hopelessness, or will our chapter be written from the realization of truth, love, courage, hope, kindness, and forgiveness?

The truth is that we all can write our verse and chapter in the book of life. The choices and freedom to write our verse and chapter are ours! As for me, I have a great example in my daughter Krista. Her chapter will live forever as a chapter of unyielding courage, love, kindness, truth, transparency, and light. I experience tremendous joy when reading her chapter, but fully realize that the chapter I write is mine to write and will depend fully on my choices and how I navigate the stresses and hardships of what's to come. *What Krista's chapter and life provide are encouragement and hope—the realization that we are worthy and life itself has tremendous value regardless of our circumstances.*

Valuable Lessons Learned:
- *Sometimes our consciousness can be extremely clear on what to do, but our emotions are the ones lagging needing a forum of expression.*
- *The fight for control is futile and nonexistent.*
- *There is incredible value in being alive and in having an individual identity with the freedom to create and choose our actions and attitudes.*
- *What Krista's chapter and life provide are encouragement and hope—the realization that we are worthy and life itself has tremendous value regardless of our circumstances.*

Chapter 21
Finding Truth

Krista had a wonderful relationship with our dog, Coco. A daily routine would entail Krista lying with Coco on our bed. They would get so close that their little heads would unite while they slept. What beautiful memories! Coco still enters Krista's room searching for her essence. Maybe she can still feel her essence and spirit!

The idea that humans need to know or feel the essence of God is an interesting one. ***Krista followed without having to know that she was*** *following. Her walk and spirit did the following naturally.* I stand to wonder if we complicate things by struggling to know or professing to know the ways of God. Can we follow God naturally within our spirit and get closer to our Creator this way? It seems that the greatest problems of life relate to people, whether Muslim, Jewish, Christian, Hindu, or other thinking that they have the true meaning of God on their side. With this approach, the leaders of these religious groups can influence others by professing to know God's word, intent, will, and judgment. People belonging to these groups are sometimes moved in different directions out of fear or the scary thought of falling outside of their perceived security of God.

It seems that people are coded with the need to believe in something in order to handle the storms of life and find some sort of security. The question is, as I see it, is there another way to walk in God's presence through one's spirit without the influence of religious groups or formal institutions? I think Krista's life answers this question. There is a way to do this if we are naturally attuned to God's presence and the spirit within us. I guess the choice will always be yours to make. I have found that in life our mind and consistent thought patterns and perceptions can resonate into creating either healthy mental frames or destructive ones.

When we examine the concept of our mind, we quickly realize that *the mind doesn't really define our identity and being*. As an example, a person can feel very good about themselves one day due to being highly praised by their fellow coworkers and supervisor. If that individual was praised for being intelligent, his/her mind begins to create thoughts and a mental frame pertaining to how intelligent they are. If this person already possessed positive affirmations about his intelligence in the past, the thoughts and perceptions created are even more cemented into a mental frame. If the same person received negative comments from his or her peers and supervisor, the person could very easily fall into the trap of believing he or she is not intelligent.

The trap is not the negative comments, but how our mind frames them and what kind of value we give them. In both examples, the person was never measured to obtain his or her intelligent quotient (IQ) or emotional intelligence (EI) levels. The person's concept of being intelligent or not was based on their created thought patterns and the frame of mind attached. The truth of how intelligent they truly are was not important to the mind in this example. Once the mind created the frame through a consistent bombardment of thoughts and perceptions, the person erroneously believed that he or she was or was not intelligent.

Once this frame gets converted in the mind as a belief, the mind falsely creates the illusion of permanency to the belief created.

The sad truth is that once the mind creates this state of erroneous permanency, the person, if not careful, can live their entire life trapped within this untruth or false frame. The term *self-fulfilling prophecy* points to this phenomenon. **From my humble observation, our value and internal worth (that include God-given natural talents) can never be changed regardless of what erroneous frames we believe about ourselves. What is will always be there.** What I do see is that if we are not careful, individuals can block these natural talents, self-worth, and value to the point of not seeing them at all. The fact that we can't see them does not imply that they are not there. It is almost like the example of a full eclipse of the sun. The sun exists whether we see it or not. There are countless persons throughout history (Einstein to name one) that at one point in their lives experienced the world around them thinking they could not amount to anything valuable due to how society defined their learning disabilities. Imagine the travesty for humanity if Einstein would have believed these erroneous frames. I am sure at one point in his life Einstein (his mind) must have battled these demons (faulty thoughts and frame) in order not to be trapped by a falsely created mental frame or belief.

As I see it the mind is a huge storage device or hard drive, a sort of giant reservoir of thoughts and experiences. We never stop placing items in this storage device as long as we live. The problem occurs when the mind gets attached to a thought and experience, creating a false identity of who we are. Once attached, the mind attempts to define us as this experience or thought. ***Looking at the mind and thoughts this way, it seems that the secret to liberating ourselves from an unhealthy pattern of thoughts and mental frames is to see the mind for what it is and equally important, not to allow ourselves to be attached to the thought creating a false identity or mindset.***

As previously mentioned, Krista did not allow society or anyone around her to define her self-worth and inherent value. Moreover, she gave to the world and people around her such love and genuine attention that it somehow allowed the individual a way to naturally tap into and connect with their true and inherent value. This natural exchange, seldom seen due to our minds blocking it, progresses through the falsely created mental frames and thought patterns of individuals, giving them for that moment in time (the only reality we have is the moment) a sense of inner security and peace of mind. What Krista could do naturally, at least for that moment, is penetrate the person's mind in order to alter and free the individual from their false perception of their self-worth. *I believe that the individuals Krista touched, from an unconscious or possibly a spiritual level, felt secure about the exchange and were able to truly see for a moment in time their internal self-worth, a God-given value communicated through the vehicle of unconditional love.* It is as if Krista, in that moment, provided them an antidote to combat their negative and faulty mental frames, the very erroneous perceptions hampering their ability to find peace of mind. I am fortunate and honored to be her father. **There is no greater value in life than to be an active participant in the greater good.** *In Krista's case, she was an active participant in erasing falsely created negative* *frames in individuals, so they could once again feel the beauty of non-judgmental love.*

Valuable Lessons Learned:

- *Krista followed without having to know that she was following. Her walk and spirit did the following naturally.*
- *The mind doesn't really define our identity and being.*
- *From my humble observation, our value and internal worth (that include God-given natural talents) can never be changed regardless of what erroneous frames we believe about ourselves. What is will always be there.*
- *Looking at the mind and thoughts this way, it seems that the secret to liberating ourselves from an unhealthy pattern of thoughts and mental frames is to see the mind for what it is and equally important, not to allow ourselves to be attached to the thought creating a false identity or mindset.*
- *There is no greater value in life than to be an active participant in the greater good.*

Chapter 22
Everyone Can Make a Small Difference

Krista never judged anyone or looked at an individual's scars in any negative manner. She was the embodiment of unconditional love. I remember Krista touching my dad's face without any concern for his condition. If people acted more like Krista, the world would be a better place!

I am sitting on a plane on my way to Costa Rica. A gentleman born in 1947 is sitting next to me. I know his date of birth because I had to help him fill out his immigration and customs paperwork. He appeared disheveled and his speech was slurred. He informed me that he was a professional gambler and was going to Costa Rica with two other friends for some fun. He mentioned how he liked beautiful women and had heard that he could see some in Costa Rica. I quickly went inside myself but stopped before my mind started to create any judgmental frames.

As we continued to talk, he told me that his dad had died at the age of ninety-four and fought in WWII. He recalled how his dad saved a battalion from getting massacred by the Japanese. The gentleman further mentioned that he had fought in Vietnam and had been exposed to Agent

Orange causing a variety of ailments. He also informed me that he had diabetes and high blood pressure. He noted that he had stopped drinking due to diabetes. Moreover, he commented that he was going to focus on having a good time with the life he had left to live. I mention this story because *in life it is always unwise to pass judgment; one will always lack information about the person, making the judgment on the individual unfair and ignorant.*

From my optic, and within the content of one's personality, a person must try to do the best they can with the situation confronted. In my case, I helped someone fill out his paperwork, shared my lunch with him, and had a small conversation with him. As one of his friends passed by our seat, he introduced me to him and in a very sincere manner commented that I had helped him and was a very nice gentleman. Was I really a nice gentleman, or did I just connect to my real self? The real self, inside every one of us, is infused by our Creator and ready to be initiated if we allow ourselves to see it.

As I analyze the situation, I remember something small but deep stirring inside me, something that told me to be open to the situation. *The way I see it, I was not a nice gentleman; I simply connected to my real self for a moment of time and made situations for someone carrying a heavy load a little bit easier.* I am learning to do this more, but at times the subject seems to be elusive. In looking at this situation the words of the Hebrew writings and Jesus are quite relevant: *"The Lord is One, Love your God with all your heart, with all your soul, with all your mind, and with all your strength. Love your neighbor as you love yourself. There is no greater commandment than these."*

Valuable Lessons Learned:
- *In life it is always unwise to pass judgment; one will always lack information about the person, making the judgment on the individual unfair and ignorant.*
- *Within the content of one's personality, a person must try to do the best they can with the situation confronted.*
- *The way I see it, I was not a nice gentleman; I simply connected to my real self for a moment of time and made situations for someone carrying a heavy load a little bit easier.*

Chapter 23
Inner Reflections

Imagine for a moment if you could describe the essence and character traits of a perfect human being. What essence would this person possess? Perhaps you would imagine this person to have a natural sense of wholeness and spiritual completeness. Moreover, it would make perfect sense that this natural wholeness and spiritual completeness would block out any act of malicious intent associated with both thought and action. And where would you find this person? Would this person need to be dependent on the perfect intellect with several advanced degrees from an Ivy League university? How about the perfect physique?

As I see it from my humble optic, **the essence needed to find perfection is found when the human spirit (divine creation) naturally exists perfectly integrated with the mind and body (thoughts and actions).** Strangely enough and contrary to popular opinion, this perfect integration does not restrict in any manner one of our most priceless gifts, our gift of freedom. **The spirit and mind are totally free and flawlessly integrated to coexist in perfect harmony.** When this integration freely and naturally occurs (not a facade or forced desire), it produces a synergistic effect altering our every thought and action. This synergistic effect, if left to its natural and divine inclination, produces a perfect and unaltered love. And this perfect and unaltered love represents here on earth the very language and essence of God.

Krista innately possessed this ability and in my humble estimation, it is what makes her a great soul. When all is said and done, I cannot bring my daughter back to physical life, but what I can do is connect to her essence and spirit. Most importantly, I will learn from her essence and channel my thoughts and actions through the power and spirit of God and unconditional love.

Valuable Lessons Learned:

- *The essence needed to find perfection is found when the human spirit (divine creation) naturally exists perfectly integrated with the mind and body (thoughts and actions).*
- *The spirit and mind are totally free and flawlessly integrated to coexist in perfect harmony.*

Acknowledgments

The Krista Marie Touch of Love Charity Inc. is a labor of love to help children diagnosed with autism. We work directly with public and private schools that provide life-saving education and therapies to autistic children. The Foundation also works with the parents of autistic children who are doing their best to deal emotionally with their present reality, in at times what can seem like a very cruel world. A percentage of the proceeds of this book will go directly to the Krista Marie

Touch of Love Charity Inc. (https://krista-marietouchoflovecharity.org) a non-profit organization dedicated to enhancing the quality of life of children with autism and other related diagnoses.

Krista-Marie's essence and legacy:
To Truly **Live** each moment
To genuinely **Love** the world around us
To joyfully **Laugh** to make a difference
And enjoy **Life** to its fullest

It is impossible to thank all the individuals that have been a part of Krista's life. I know deep in my heart that for them their greatest blessing is to have been able to experience Krista's unconditional love and transferrable joy. I am very grateful for the assistance and guidance provided by Glenn and Bryan Balch. Laurick Ingram, thank you for supporting my family through this journey. To my daughter Katrina, thank you for your unending love and courage throughout the years. My niece Julie Gonzalez for her support, friendship, love, and beautiful design of the cover. Most of all I must thank my beautiful wife and soulmate, Marta. It is impossible to describe the amount of strength, courage, and unconditional love displayed by her. Krista's essence and spirit truly radiate in her heart. Marta, it is truly a privilege to be your husband, and eternal friend!

Dad following in Krista's footsteps

Krista and her sister Katrina

Mom remembering Krista

ABOUT THE AUTHORS

Dr. Bernardo Gonzalez and his wife Marta Gonzalez are the eternally grateful parents of Krista-Marie.

THE END

www.ingramcontent.com/pod-product-compliance
Lightning Source LLC
LaVergne TN
LVHW051557070426
835507LV00021B/2621